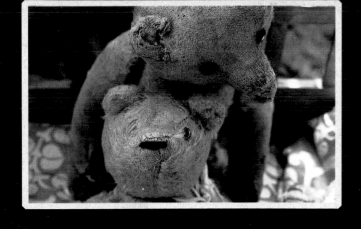

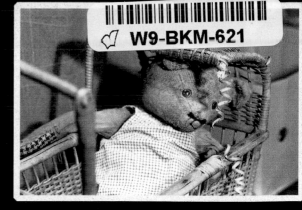

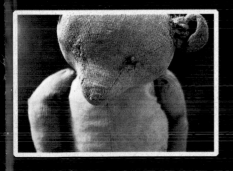

Teddy's World

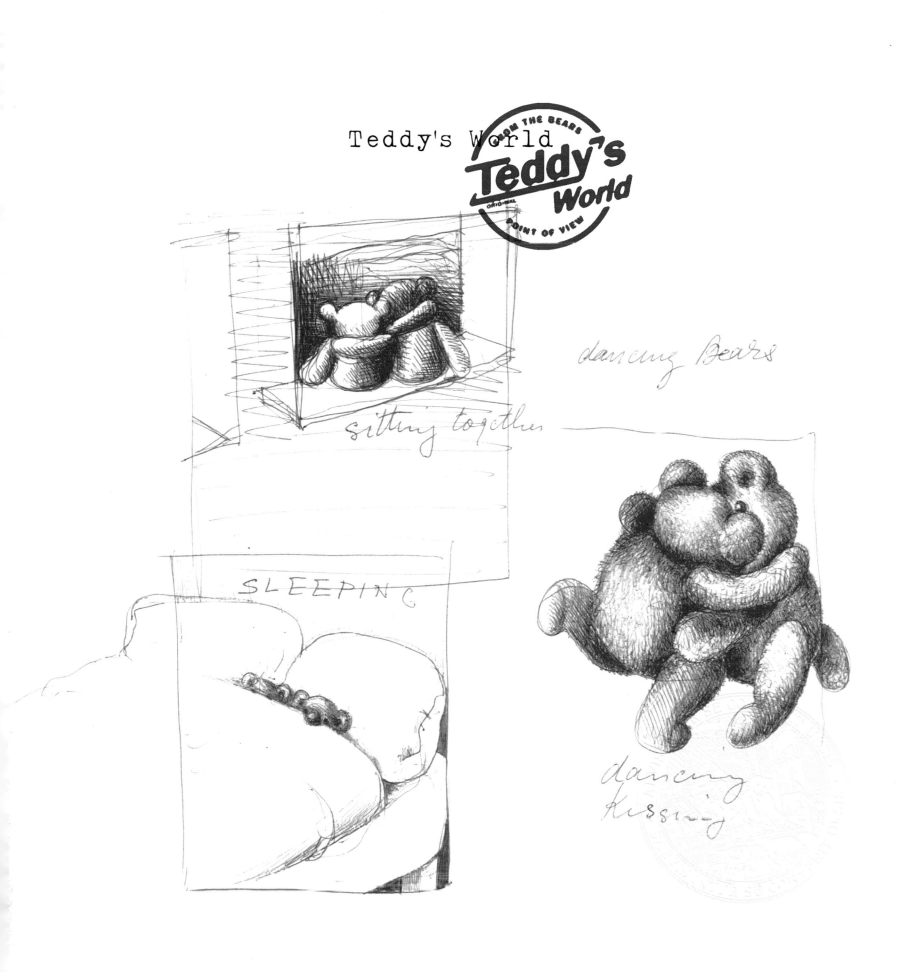

dancing Bears

sitting together

SLEEPING

dancing
kissing

World

A JOOST ELFFERS BOOK

Joost Elffers Books/Teddy's World LLC
In association with SGP
225 Lafayette St.
New York, NY 10012

Library of Congress Cataloging-in-Publication Data

Vries, Mirja de.
  Teddy's world / by Mirja de Vries and Joost Elffers.
    p. cm.
  ISBN 0-9718975-0-6
  1. Teddy bears. I. Elffers, Joost. II. Title.
  NK8740 .V75 2002
  745.592'43--dc21

                              2002005385

Printed in Germany

Introduction

We bears are given to children long before they are able to recognize us. As a result, sometimes a most precious bear huddles in a corner, while a favorite blanket, a little ball or even a rubber duck gets all the attention. So, we just sit there on the shelf, patiently waiting until we become the chosen one to go out on an intimate journey with the child. This book opens up the world of teddy bears with pictures, like a dream recalling your own memories. Every day, in every way, and everywhere you go, you see the intense relationship between us and children. That's the wonder of our having been – for a hundred years already – the favorite travel guides of small children as they explore the world that very rapidly is growing ever larger all around them. No one can interfere with the bond between teddy and child. And the journey on which we embark is one filled with play, fantasy, creativity and a large dose of reality.

For us, the child is the one who sets the rules of the game, and parents should keep their hands off. If absolutely necessary, they may step in to make repairs on us, but only with our companion's consent. It is always best that nothing about us be altered.

Generally, we are on rather formal terms with the parents. We don't fully understand what they expect of us. If they wash us, horrendous things can happen. Our relationship can be terribly shaken, and we are afraid that our little friends will not be able to smell us and recognize us anymore.

What does Mother really want from us? Though it should be said, in all honesty, that we become unbelievably dirty at times, to the point of being truly disgusting.

At the peak of the relationship, our influence within the family is enormous. Because of our size, it can sometimes be inconvenient to take us to the park or on vacation, but we are rarely left behind. Everyone is scared to death that the child will make a terrible scene, or worse, that we'll get lost. In that sense, we browbeat them all into submission and occupy our well-deserved and rightful place as long as it lasts.

If, at the end of this journey, the child is done with us and is able to move on alone, then we are left behind to be stuck up on the highest shelf of a closet or given away. The child doesn't always mourn this separation, but rarely forgets us completely. The experiences we have shared and the things we have lived through together are carried along into adulthood, even if we are no longer present to offer concrete proof. Usually, we lose the central spot in the development of our dearest and only friend. If we age well and preserve our wonderful appearance, we continue to serve as a memory of bygone times. We come to life thanks to children. Without this intense relationship, we remain bears, but don't really live. Our dependency may seem disconcerting or pathetic, but we have no other way of being. We are who we are!

The Mirror Of Love

The teddy bear's task is to mirror love. We are good at that. What you give us, we return. We are good listeners, we see everything, are most trustworthy, and never let our tongue run away with us. We are not judgmental. We're simply there for those who are attracted to us and always unconditionally so.

We are depositories for memories. Like a battery, we can store what is solid and good and give it back when things are bad or when emotional needs must be met. If you want to talk about faithfulness, you need only think of us. The loyalty of a dog is nothing compared to ours. And we exist in greater numbers. Teddy bears live with people in almost every home, in just about every country in the world. There may well be a billion bears, all doing their work in their own way: mirroring love, lending an ear, handing out bear hugs. We are sent out on missions of comfort and solace. We help sick children during hard times and are great experts where loneliness is concerned. We try to remedy the feeling of abandonment or loss, whether a child is alone at a boarding school or during a stay with a distant relative. Whenever the environment is unfamiliar or frightening, we step in to fill that chilly void. And don't think this stops with children. When needed, we simply stay around.

Sometimes, years later, when a child is an adult and gone from home, Mother will come upon us and look into our eyes, and she will see standing there, big as life, her little child and our old friend.

Where Do I Come From?

There are so many stories about where teddy bears come from. One time, I heard about a hard-working man and his wife, *Morris* and *Rose Michtom*, who owned a small candy shop in Brooklyn, New York. One day, they learned about how President Teddy Roosevelt had spared a bear cub while hunting in the wilderness, and they saw a picture of the baby bear in the papers and were inspired to create us. They placed this special bear in the window of their store, calling it "Teddy's Bear." Everyone who saw it said, "I want one, too!" The Michtoms worked day and night and needed so many people to help make bears that they became the IDEAL factory, producing bears for all America.

There is another story that the first bear was made in Germany. A saintly German woman named *Margarete Steiff* made wonderful felt toys for children, especially her six nephews and three nieces. One day her nephew Richard showed her some drawings he made of bears at the zoo, and she put her magical needle to a piece of golden mohair and created us. When Richard took this beautiful bear to the Leipzig toy fair, everybody wanted one, and very soon, the Steiff factory was making teddy bears for the whole world! In England, they say that Crown Prince Edward, nicknamed "Teddy" by those who loved him, inspired the first British bear. In France the first bear was called Nounours, after a character in a children's book. There is a different version in Russia and yet another story of origin in Japan.

A literal bear garden

Who am I?

I am the child's very first friend. Although I am a child myself, I am also part of the great big world. As we go on our journey, and I see the world, I start asking questions, too. All little bears, as they grow up, wonder, "Who am I?"

We looked at bears in nature and were amazed by them: the Polar Bear swimming in the Arctic Ocean, the Brown Bear soaking in a pool of water. We even thought we had to learn to swim until we saw the great Grizzly Bear who rules the Rocky mountains. Nature's bears look huggable, but in reality they are very dangerous. Although we are bears, we are not like them! We are soft and huggable outside, but firm on the inside. We have evolved from being a four-footed creature, like our companions who also started by crawling. Even without a skeleton, we can stand up and walk on our own two feet.

When we visited the Museum, we saw depicted in a mosaic how the ancient Romans baited bears just for fun. As we walked through the galleries, we learned how we inspired paintings by old masters.
Have you ever seen bears dancing in a forest glen or the pandemonium of bears and bulls in the Market of bygone days? At last, we came to the Teddy Bear Portrait Gallery, which exhibits the culmination of our evolution, celebrating our unique beauty, charm, dignity and character. We have witnessed our own proud history: we are necessary to mankind!

It makes you wonder, could a child ever become a complete person without first learning to love his bear? In giving life to us, the child imagines his own humanity. He starts to see life in objects and learns to share and to appreciate the beauty of others. It's the bear who shows a child that there is life and meaning outside of himself. And he "grows up" only by learning this about the world. Then, everything starts falling into perspective. When the child finally understands that we are teddy bears, simply cherished toys, then the child becomes a mature person.

We were inspired by nature's bear but created by a human need that made us Teddy Bears.

Is that what they call **bearish behavior?**

This proves it: *all bears live in the water.*

ALASKA BROWN BEAR
GIFT OF

Bears a striking resemblance...

Teddies come in all shapes
and sizes now, but in the first half
of the last century, we looked more like
live bears. We had longer snouts and smaller
ears. And now these bears have something
else in common with us,
they're *stuffed*, too!

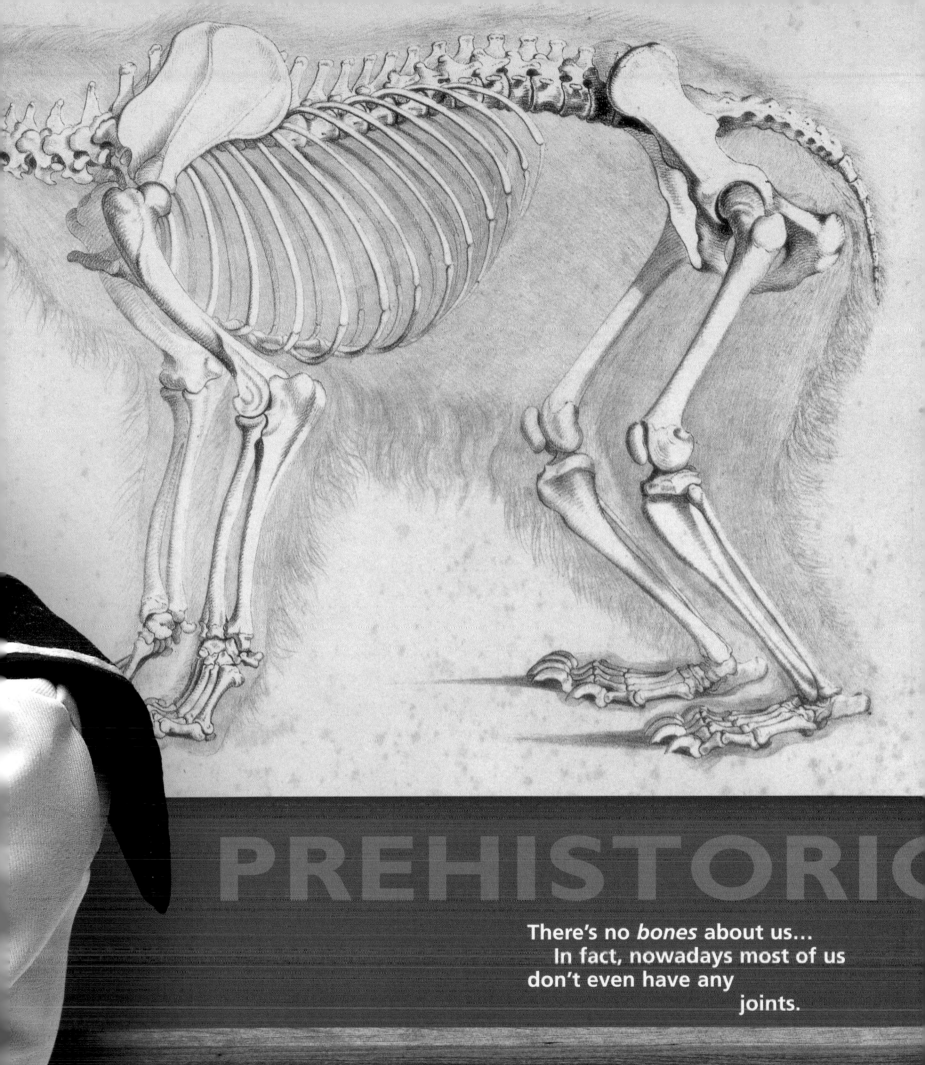

PREHISTORIC

There's no *bones* about us...
In fact, nowadays most of us
don't even have any
joints.

TEXTILES

Teddy
Bear
Textiles

TEXTILES

Bears in A...

ORSO MOSAICA

...rs... mosaica:
Bears in
Ancient Times

NOW OPEN

"Bear Baiting"

Roman Mosaic Depicting Circus Games

The Bear Dance
William H. Beard. Oil, 1879

"What can be so bad about a *Bear Market*?"

Bulls and Bears in the Market
William H. Beard. Oil, 1879

a **confirming** moment

"Bears comparison, don't you think?"

The Night Watch
Rembrandt. Oil, 1642

We do have fears: getting lost, being left out in the rain, landing in the jaws of a dog. Even being stored away somewhere can become hazardous after a while. Dust isn't too bad, but dampness poses a real threat. We can get moldy and rot. The older we get, the more we fear being too close to a garbage can.

But the worst of it often comes in the teenage years. Our companions begin to lose interest. They don't seem to need or want us anymore, or they're embarrassed by us. The mothers might even give us away like hand-me-down clothes! Or we get packed away in a box, stuffed in the back of a closet, shut up in the attic. It's the end of the affair – and that'll take a toll.

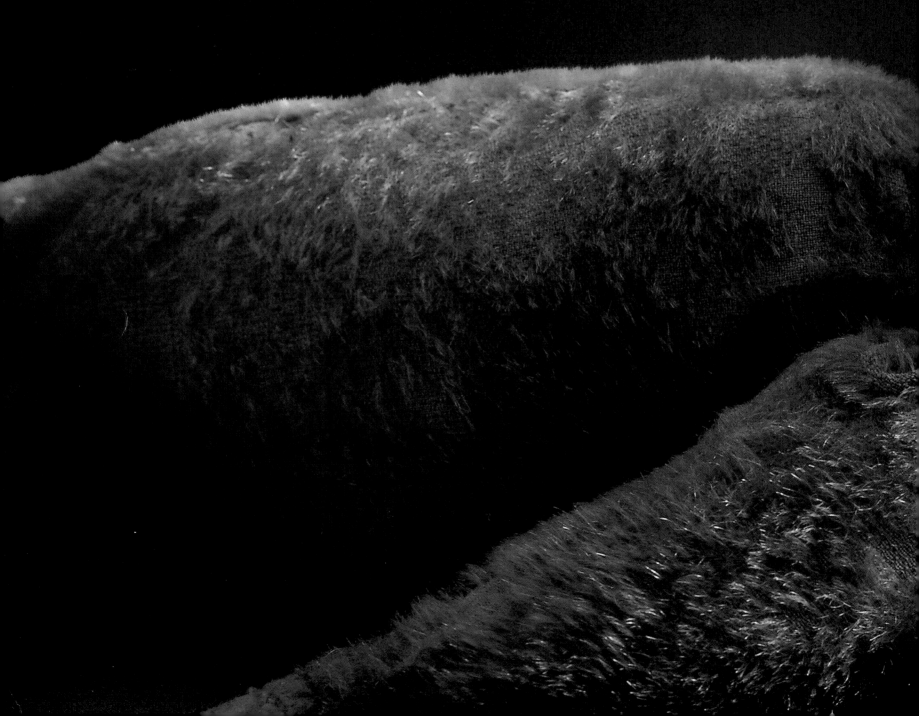

Bear in Mind...

It's all so hard to bear.

The end of the affair

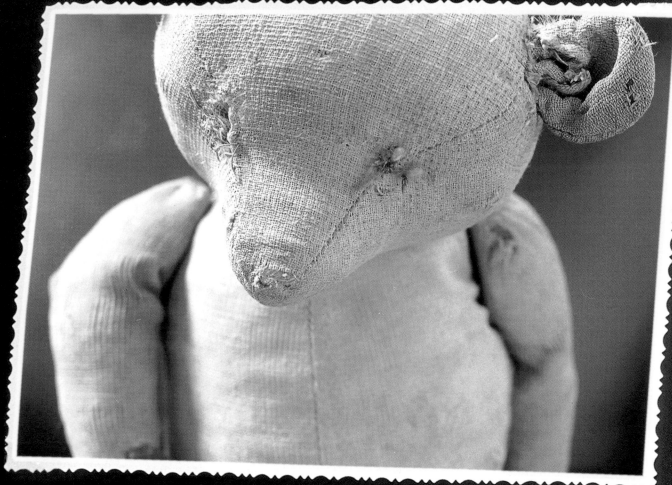

Memories in black and white

Bear Hugs Abound!

The Right to Bear Arms

It's no longer a politics of right or left. Bears everywhere are demonstrating for the right to arm themselves. "What could we do without arms?" they point out. "We seek no restrictions on our right to bear arms, to keep them on our person, obviously, and to move about freely with them, as necessary."

"Up in arms"

CLASSIFIEDS

REAL ESTATE
Vacation Properties/
Country Estates

Mountainside. Dramatic Den! One of a kind contemporary. Magnificent views, dramatic windows, cathedral style ceilings, several skylights. Directions: take Lake Rd. to Sunny Slope. Tel: 555-1918
New to Market! Rustic Relaxation. Great location on Lookout Post Rd. Light, bright, open floor plan. Deck, patio, spectacular views! Adjacent to Nature Preserve. Directions: take Rt.2 West to Lookout Post exit. Bear left, Tel: 555-1492

CARTOONS

" I shouldn't, but I'm going to have the garbage"

" I never realized they had feelings"

B-2-B CONTACTS

Bear-to-Bear Personals

Everybody needs a hug — and bear hugs seem to be the best of the bunch. In fact, no one is better at giving hugs than teddy bears. They are the quintessential comforters, and now it seems teddy bears are fast becoming synonymous with "goodwill."

Perhaps this is a result of our profound ability to mirror love. But whatever the cause, bear hugs are symptomatic of the great need everyone has for love, affection and comfort.

This comforting nature extends well beyond our role as devoted childhood companions. As far back as 1912, when the Steiffs dressed some teddies entirely in black to mourn the Titanic tragedy, we've come to be regarded as nurturers, caregivers, and providers of solace. In 1951, teddy bears were officially introduced into hospitals to comfort and cheer sick children. And in 1973, the international humanistic organization "Good Bears of the World," was

founded, expanding on the idea of calling upon teddy bears to benefit sick or needy children everywhere. And it makes sense: few things can make a child smile like we can. In fact, bearing goodwill is what we do best.

Over time, our goodwill work began to move out of the strictly private world and more and more into the public sphere — coming to the rescue not only of the sick, but of those distressed and distraught by tragedy or disaster.

In 1996, teddy bears became integral to the fundraising efforts to benefit the children and families devastated by the earthquake in Kobe, Japan.

In 1997, when Princess Diana was killed in a fatal car accident, so many mourners looked to us to help them through their sadness and grief, and to remain at the site of her former home, keeping her memory alive.

Most recently, we have found ourselves sitting together, by the thousands, near Ground Zero after the World Trade Center

tragedy of 9-11. We are keeping vigil, in a way, helping families and friends honor the precious memories of so many loved and lost.

Who would have ever thought that we would come so far? That the teddy bears' role would be so significant and so widespread? It is a development that bears further reflection — both by teddy bears and those who love us so,

Everybody needs a hug — and bear hugs are the best of the bunch.

Woodhaven, Call this cave home! Escape the hustle and bustle. This cozy little cave on a quiet country lane is a perfect place to get away and hibernate. Located on the South Slope. For info and appointment, call: 555-2513.

Glorious Getaway! Perfect for Romantic Weekends! Exquisite outdoor bath with large sunken tub. Skylights. Wall of windows with mountain views! By appointment only. Call: 555-2855

Culture Cub! Stylish, refined yet full of fun. Looking for friend who'll enjoy the finer things: ballroom bear dancing, smoked salmon brunches, and

Cute & Cuddly. Soft, romantic, stay-at-home bear seeks same for cozy evenings cuddling on the couch. Must be gentle and mature, with a good sense of humor. Photo appre-

---

Berryman cartoon in Washington Post, Nov.16, 1902

Important Dates in Teddy Bear History

Morris Michtom

1902 Teddy Bears are conceived in the United States and Germany, by the Michtoms and the Steiffs respectively
1903 Bears are a hit. Michtoms start Ideal Novelty & Toy Co. in Brooklyn, NY; Steiff gets an order for 3000 at the Leipzig Toy Fair
1904 President "Teddy" Roosevelt adopts the Teddy Bear as official campaign mascot; it had been the moose
1905 Seymour Eaton's Roosevelt Bears, "Teddy G." & "Teddy B" appear for first time
1906 Teddy Bear mania in the USA and Europe. Many manufacturers spring up. Steiff has dispatched over a million bears by 1907
1907 Steiff declares this the "Year of the Bear." Tune that will become known as "Teddy Bear's Picnic" is composed by J.F. Stratton. Lyrics written in 1930 by Jimmy Kennedy
1910–1917 England joins in Teddy Bear Boom. Bears become integral to toy production throughout Europe and USA. It's all the fashion for children to be photographed with teddies
1912 Teddy Bears are recognized in Carl Jung's theory of psychoanalysis
1912 Steiff bears wear black to mourn the sinking of the Titanic
1917 Alfonzo leaves Russia for London
1919 A Teddy Bear makes the first non-stop trans-Atlantic flight accompanied by Alcock

---

1920 Rupert Bear appears in the Daily Express and continues to for almost 70 years
1921 The Farnell Co. Teddy that will inspire Winnie-the-Pooh comes to the home of Christopher Robin Milne
1926 A.A. Milne takes readers into the 100 Acre Woods to meet Winnie-the-Pooh
1920s–1930s Many more novelty Teddy Bears are created, especially by Schuco and Bing. These musical and mechanical bears walk, dance, twirl and tumble. Numerous songs about Teddy Bears become top hits
1939–1945 WWII: almost no new bears are born in Europe; birthrate also drops in the USA
1950 The bear cub rescued from a forest fire in Lincoln National Forest is dubbed "Smokey Bear" and becomes famous as the spokesbear for forest fire prevention
1951 Teddy Bears begin their goodwill work at hospitals in Ohio, with the encouragement of Mr. Russell McClea
1954 Washable Teds hit the scene. Wendy Boston's bears change the nature of Teddy Bears dramatically
1955 Col. Bob Henderson, "Teddy Girl's" original friend begins his study of the influence of Teddy Bears in the Western world
1958 Michael Bonds introduces Paddington to the world
1962 The first official Teddy Bear Club is organized
1965 A Teddy bear climbs the Matterhorn's north slope
1969 Peter Bull appears on Johnny Carson's "Tonight Show" following publication of his Teddy Bear Book. The British actor professes his lifelong fascination and affection for teddies
1973 International humanistic organization "Good Bears of the World" is founded, expanding on the earlier idea of placing teddy bears in hospitals to benefit sick children

---

1975 Mirja de Vries begins photographing teddy bears
1982 "Delicatessen" rises to television stardom playing "Aloysius" in the TV adaptation of Evelyn Waugh's 1945 novel *Brideshead Revisited*
1986 Teddy Bear museum opens in Berlin
1980s–1990s Numerous Teddy Bear Fairs and Conventions begin meeting all over the world.
1996 Teddy Bears are an integral part of the fundraising efforts to benefit children after the Kobe, Japan earthquake
2001 Teddy Bears pitch in and keep vigil after the September 11th attacks at the World Trade Center in New York
2002 Teddy Bear Centennial And that's just the 1st Century

Margarete Steiff, ca. 1900

"Teddy" cartoon by Clifford Berryman

The Da

The First Teddy Bear Newspaper   EST. 1903   The Daily Ro

Tattered Ted!

Who let this dog out? A horrifying dog attack leaves another teddy in tatters.

Each year, dog attacks result in millions of serious injuries. Although surgical procedures can usually repair the damage, obviously it would be best to prevent attacks in the first place. These tragedies should not be regarded as unpredict- able, but as preventable. Precautions can and should be taken. The level of attacks is directly connected to the level of responsibility exercised by dog owners. Dog owners can no longer live in denial. If they do, both teddies and dogs will continue to suffer. Remember, responsible pet ownership can take the bite out of the dog.

Color Blind – And Proud of It!

News media report daily about violent outbreaks due to racial tensions and clashes in other worlds. It's disturbing to hear about such incidents. It's also very confusing for us. Can it really be that color makes such a difference?

We can't imagine judging each other by the color of our mo- hair. It doesn't make sense. Ultimately it's what's inside that counts (and we're all made with pretty much the same stuff!).

Flat-Paw Investigates Foul Play!

An unidentified victim was dis- covered in the downtown area late last night. The bear (dark mohair, dark brown eyes, about 18" tall) was rushed to the hospital where he is listed

íly Roar

Thursday May 13t

Yellowstone, Cub Caverns 45548   Vol. CMII No. 100   Bear in Chief : T. B. Roosevelt

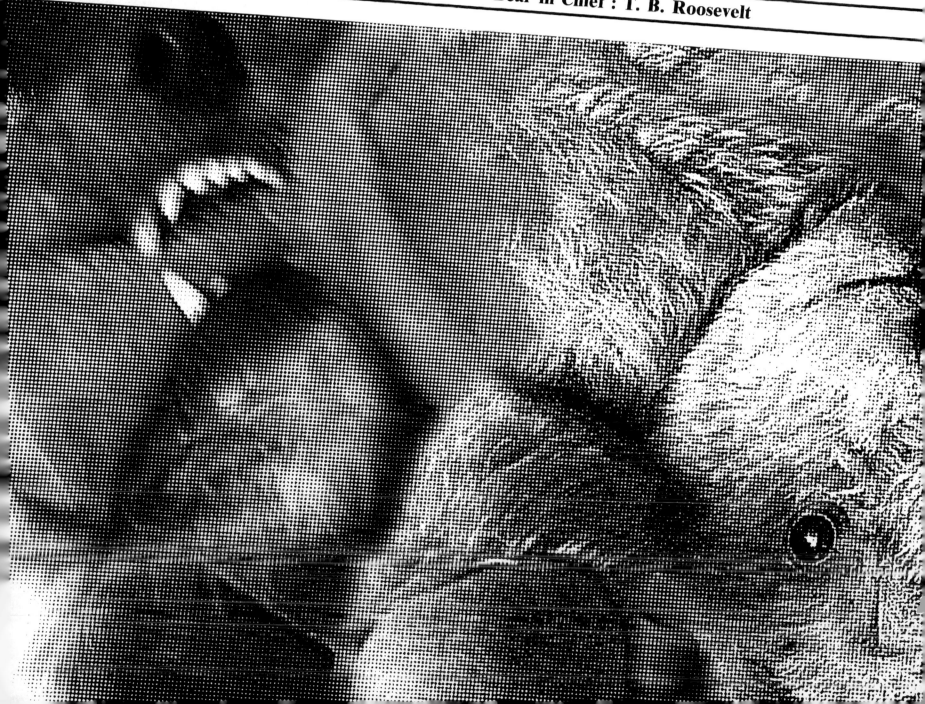

Home is where the bear is...

As we play,
we explore the whole range
of domestic activities.

The *human*
masquerade…

The entertainment can be *so* mesmerizing.

A classic magic lantern show:

"The 3 Bears and Goldilocks"

1. Mama bear made some porridge
2. The porridge was too hot
3. The bears went out for a walk while it cooled
4. Goldilocks couldn't resist
5. After lunch Goldilocks decided to take a rest
6. When the bears returned, Papa Bear noticed, "Someone's been eating our porridge."
7. "And that someone is sleeping in our beds!"
8. The bears woke her with a fright. Goldilocks took flight out the window and was never heard from again.

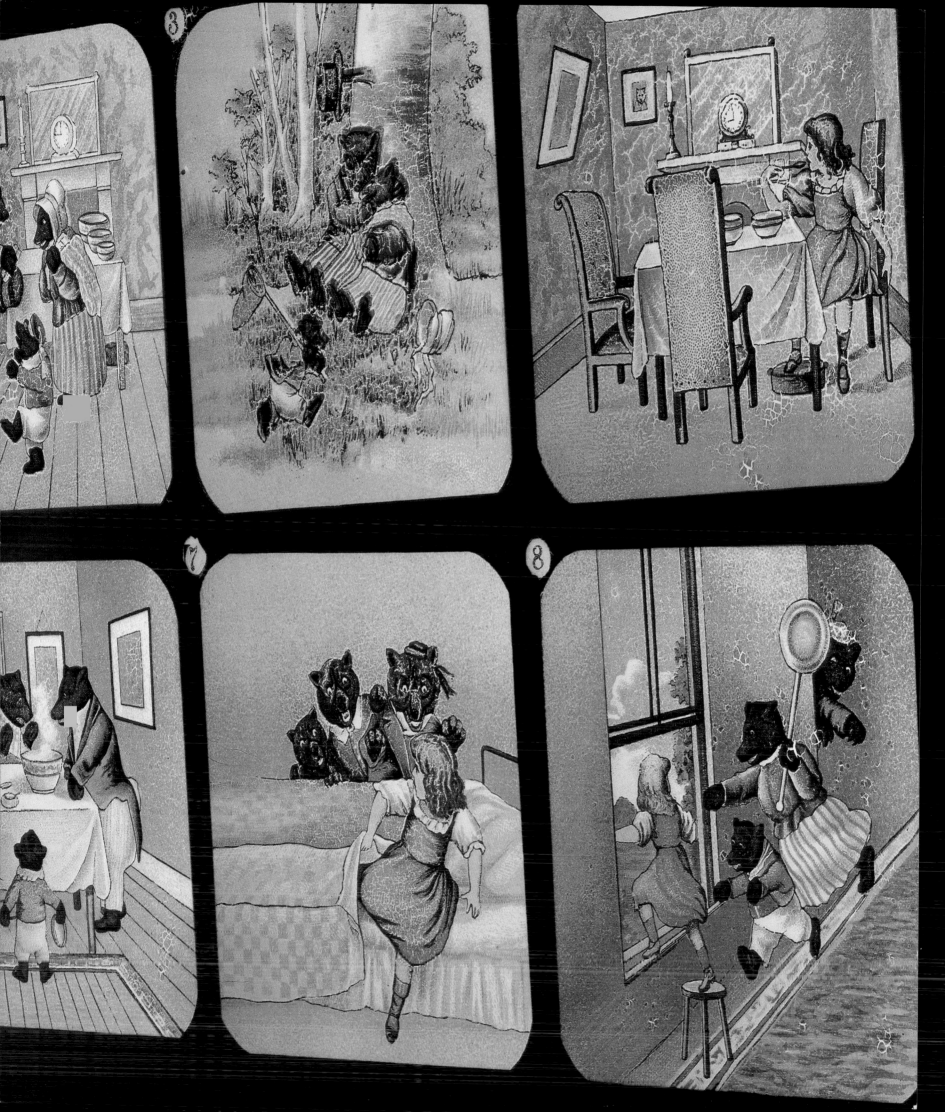

Food looms large in our companions' lives.
From mother to bottle to solids,
eating is often a huge production –
and the first taste of control.

We act it all out in frequent rehearsals.

My Dear Friend,

    She did it again. Just like before, she grabbed me,
Muttering what a stinky bear I am. It was awful.
    But at least it wasn't the washing machine.
I wouldn't have survived that a second time.

    What will become of me? Remember last time?
You were so upset. You barely recognized me
without my familiar smell, and you almost
didn't want me anymore. It took a while before
things were right between us again.

    But why does she do it? She must be jealous.
Bear with me until everything's back to the way it was.

    Teddy

    PS: I'm just glad she didn't throw the bear out with
the bath water.

Left hanging
out to *dry*

Teddy bears and bedtime stories –
a perfect match

Teddy bears exist on the very borders of fantasy and reality, of waking and sleeping. It is here, in these transitions, that our function is critical – at its most essential even. While we are fantasy characters in daylight play, *at nighttime we are very real protectors* – guiding the companion through the magic and mystery of the darkness and shadows, dreams and nightmares.

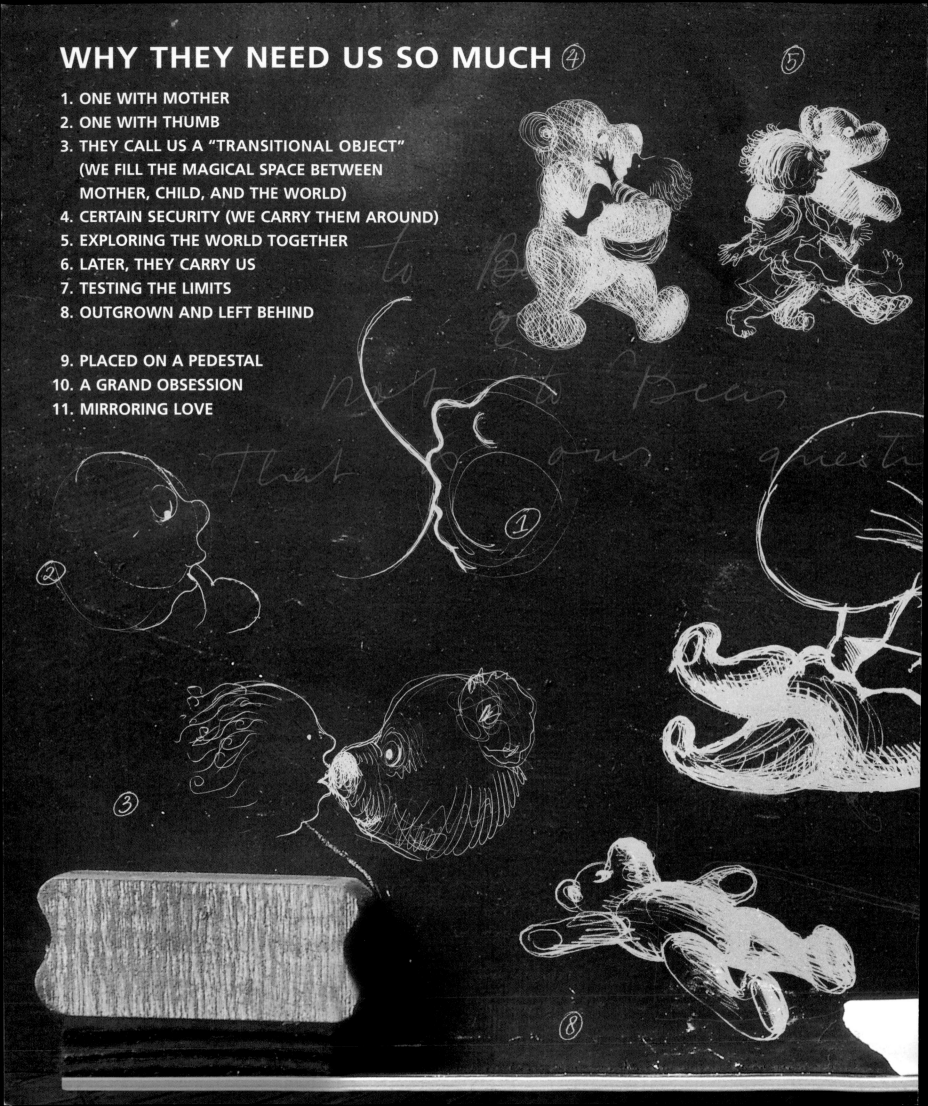

WHY THEY NEED US SO MUCH

1. ONE WITH MOTHER
2. ONE WITH THUMB
3. THEY CALL US A "TRANSITIONAL OBJECT"
   (WE FILL THE MAGICAL SPACE BETWEEN
   MOTHER, CHILD, AND THE WORLD)
4. CERTAIN SECURITY (WE CARRY THEM AROUND)
5. EXPLORING THE WORLD TOGETHER
6. LATER, THEY CARRY US
7. TESTING THE LIMITS
8. OUTGROWN AND LEFT BEHIND

9. PLACED ON A PEDESTAL
10. A GRAND OBSESSION
11. MIRRORING LOVE

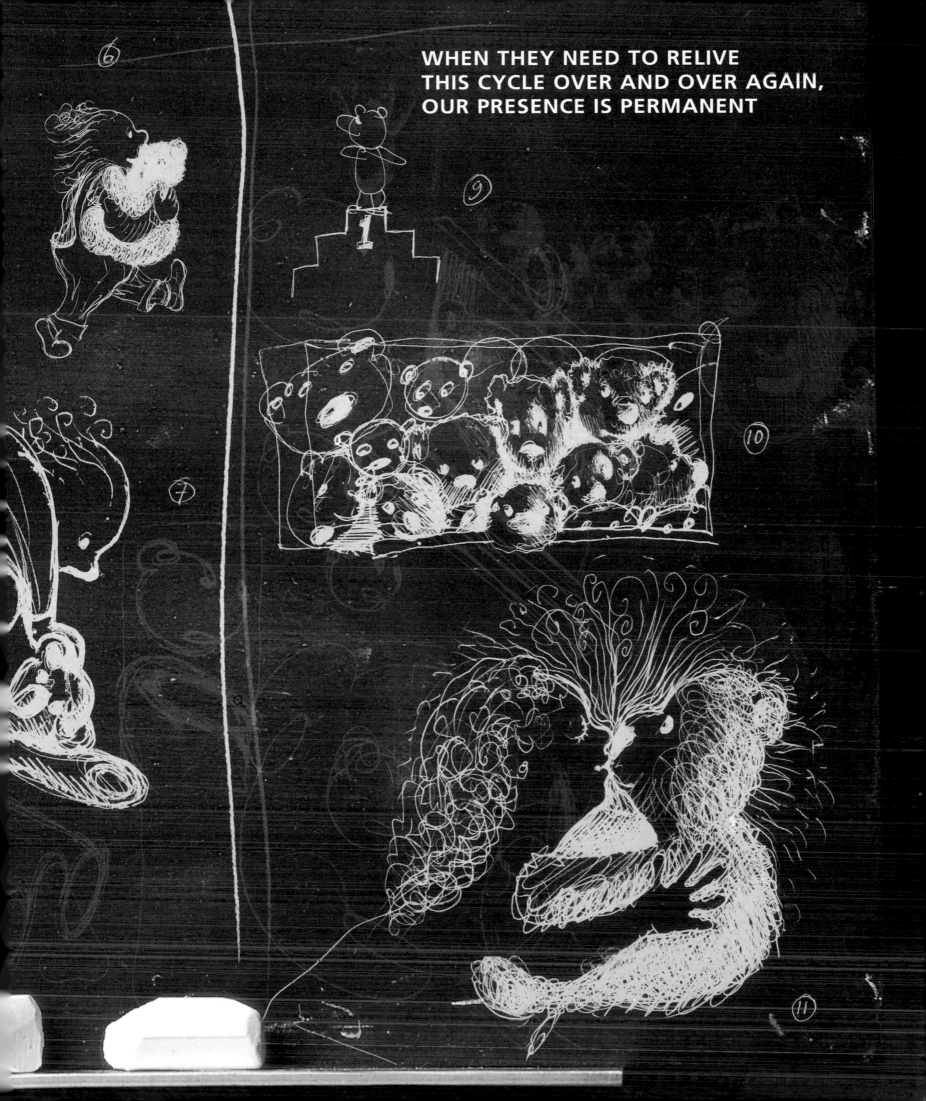

Over time,
    we got softer, rounder – and "cuter" –
proportioned more like human babies.
But is this truly natural selection?

TEDDY ORIGINS

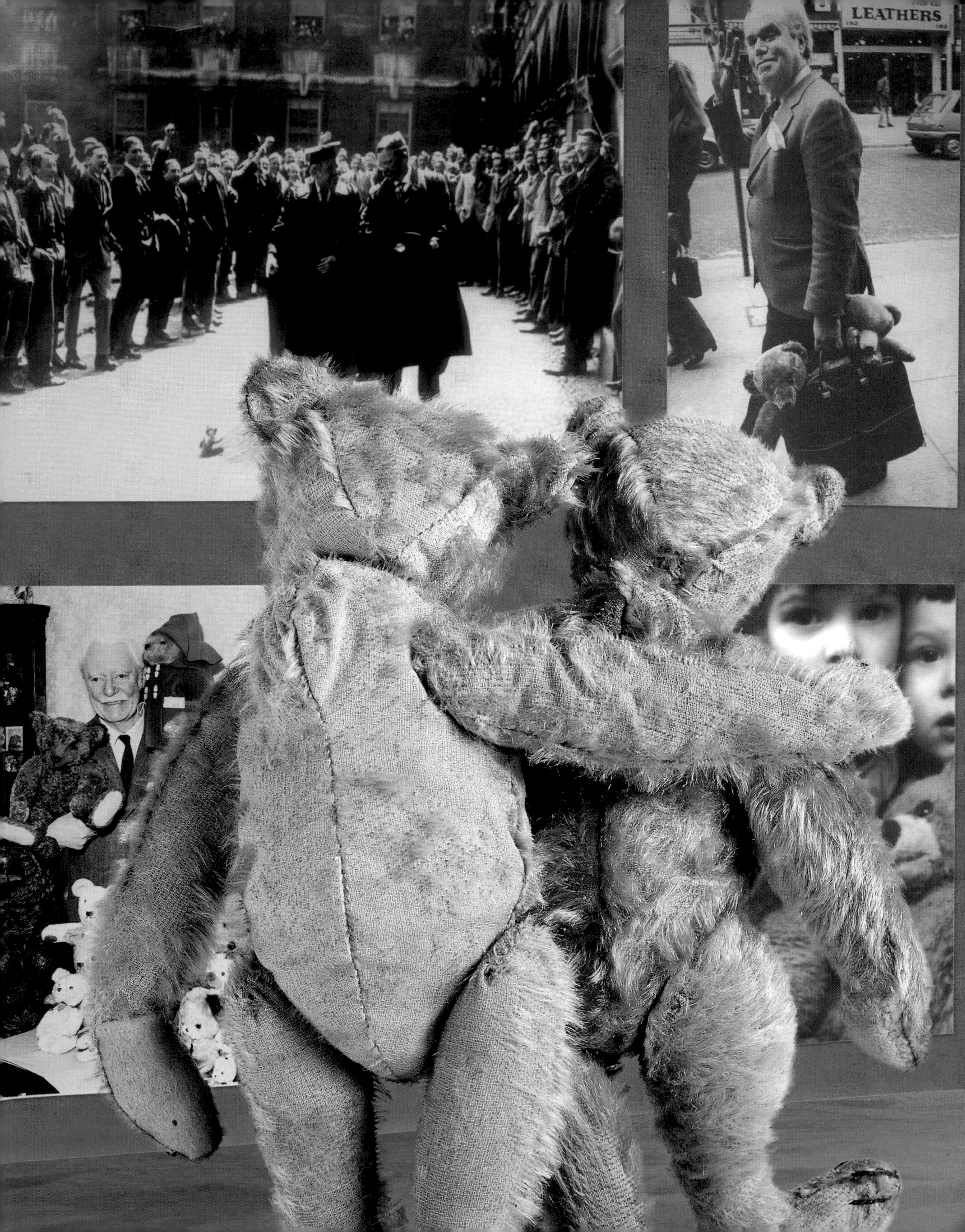

FAMOUS BEARS

XENIA
OF RUSSIA

ALFONZO'S FAMILY TREE

ALFONZO

Bear books are a vast – and enduring – genre.

The "Teddy" part is a name they found
On hat and tree and leggings round,
On belt and boot, and plates of tin,
And scraps of paper and biscuits thin,
And other things that hunters drop
When they chase a bear to a mountain top.

Their home was high and deep and wide,
An elegant place for bears to hide
The things picked up on the mountain side.
They were well supplied with hats and boots,
And leather coats and cow-boy suits,
And pots and pans and whips and strings,
And guns and horns and a hundred things
Lost on the trail by hunters bold
When driven home by the winter's cold.

10

While we love and admire those very famous bears – like Pooh and Paddington, Rupert and the Roosevelt Bears – they're not really Teddy Bears at all.
They're Literati Bears.

EIN SONNTAGS-

0129

"Two Roosevelt Bears had a home out West
In a big ravine near a mountain crest."

The Roosevelt Bears

The Roosevelt Bears – "Teddy B." and "Teddy G." – were a series of four books created by Seymour Eaton between 1905 and 1908. The curious bears travelled far and wide, enjoying many adventures – in New York, Pittsburgh and Washington DC; at West Point, a wax museum, and a zoo; they went fishing, played baseball, and even put out fires.

And their tales, told in lively, rhyming verse, helped boost the teddy bear's already growing popularity, and inspired numerous novelty items like mugs, spoons and posters. And according to Mr. Eaton, he created these characters to "teach children that… bears may have some measure of human feeling."

"TEDDY-B put a match to a pile of wood
And made a fire and cooked the food."

Teddy bears
and their companions
are incredibly **curious**.
We simply need to find
things out – and the more
we learn, the more we want
to know. It's just our nature.

**In that way, learning is like
honey for us – we're born
with a taste for it.**

A bear as a *honey pot*?

Was that an **authorized** usage?
Or are we in the public domain after 100 years?

Some bears dress up a lot.

Is a bear ever *really* barenaked?

Some even get their identity
from the clothes they bear.

BELLE

SHE-BEAR VS HE-BEAR

BEARING THE FASHIONS OF THE TIMES

BARE NECESSITIES "I HAVEN'T GOT A THING TO BEAR!"

BEAR PARTY

BEARLY DRESSED

A ROARING GOOD TIME!

BIG BEAR TARS

BEARLY *dressed*

"Rich Rags or Ragged Riches?"

The best-loved bears can end up in tatters – and turn it into a fashion statement.
Or is it the other way around?

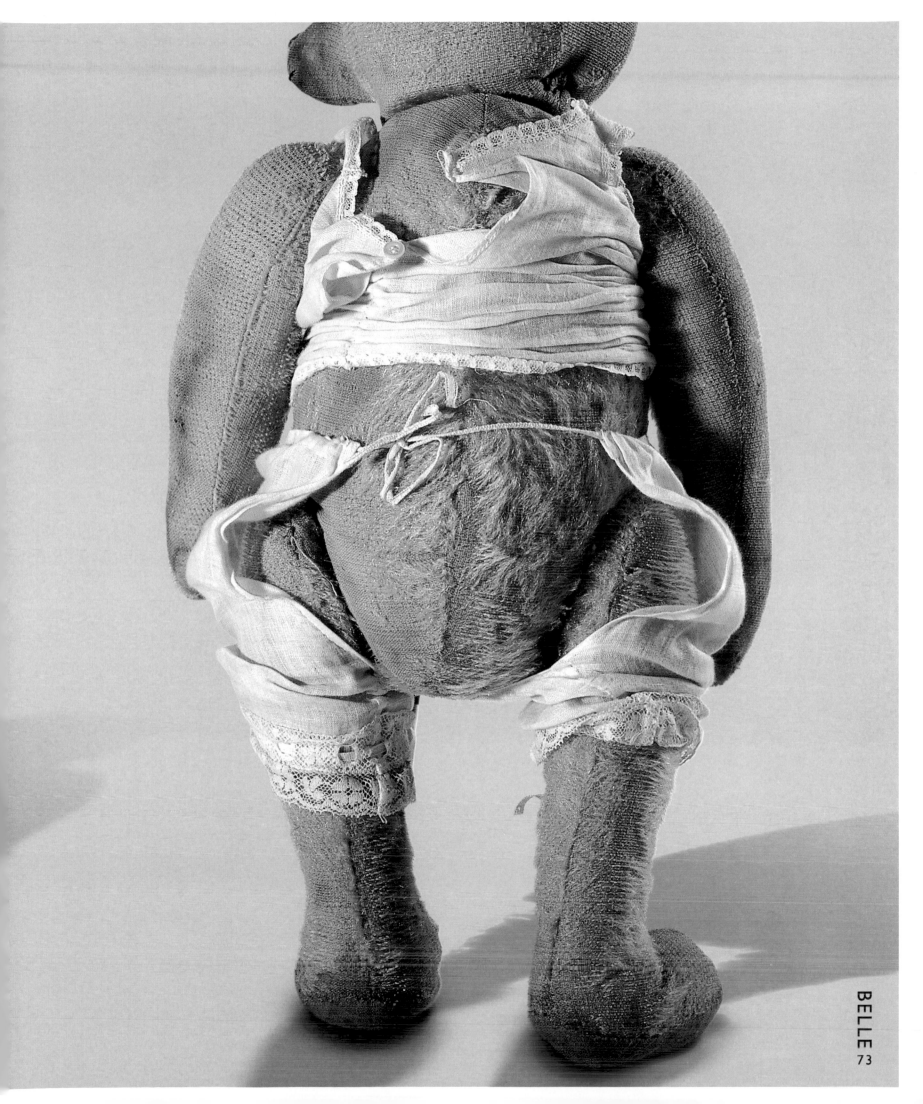

BEAR THREADS

One of this season's most sought after styles is this fun, faux fur ensemble from Orsa de Bär.

BELLE

74

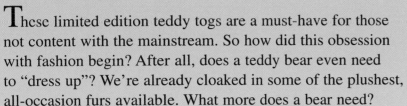

These limited edition teddy togs are a must-have for those not content with the mainstream. So how did this obsession with fashion begin? After all, does a teddy bear even need to "dress up"? We're already cloaked in some of the plushest, all-occasion furs available. What more does a bear need?

Clothes make the Bear

There are two distinct camps: those who come dressed and those who don't. And even though the fur-only fanatics sometimes play "dress up" with their companions, there is a very definite difference between the two groups: the naturally undressed, who prefer to be "pure ted," and those who get their identity from the clothes they bear. In fact, this total connection between some teddies and their clothes is so strong that it cannot be severed – even when the clothes have become worn, torn and totally out of style. These bears are literally attached to their clothes. Eventually they may be seen as "shabby chic" or end up in the yard-sale pile.

So how can a teddy pick the perfect outfit – an enduring fashion persona – when identifying with a specific outfit can make or break a bear? Once the line-dancing craze is over, how hip are the cowboy boots and 10-gallon hat? Will it be a "get it and forget it" syndrome? And what of the haute couture cubs? What happens when the designer of the moment falls out of fashion? Will these teds crawl into a cave for eternal hibernation?

Indeed, you must carefully consider which clothes to wear – if any! But first you must find your fashion ID:

Are you a purist or a dress-up devotee?

Often we have our picture taken
to become part of a collection... "Say bear!"
Sometimes
a photo is all that remains.

Name/nom:
Family/familie:
Residence/domicile:

*"There, in a collection of old photos,
I saw myself – and discovered my true identity.
I was actually **a muff**,
and the holes in my sides were not accidental."*

The *bear* facts

Name/nom: Jean Jean
Family/familie: Fadap
Residence/domicile: Mir-Amsterdam

Name/nom: Gretchen
Family/familie: Steiff 1908
Residence/domicile: Els-Bodegraven

Name/nom: Football Player
Family/familie: -
Residence/domicile: Germany(DU)

Name/nom:
Family/familie:
Residence/domicile:

Name/nom:
Family/familie: French Ted
Residence/domicile: De Vries-Amsterdam

Name/nom:
Family/f
Residenc

Name/nom: Arnold & Tim
Family/familie: Steiff 1920
Residence/domicile: Els-Bodegraven

Name/nom: Herman
Family/familie: Hermann 1920
Residence/domicile: Els-Bodegraven

Name/nom:
Family/familie:
Residence/dom

Name/no
Family/fo
Residenc

BEAR ARCHIVES

Lost since last week
who saw my paw 2 please call 30625-127
ING
4491917
Sheila is lost
Have you seen her?
357912
BILLY
last seen y
nom: Hanging Bear
amily/familie: Bing 1910
dence/domicile: Michel K

MR. EARS
S MISSING

S M please help G
sterday in this area

Have You Lost Your Bearings?

Getting lost is a serious matter.
How can it happen?
Who's to blame?
For teddy bears, day trips,
vacations, visits, all become
an occasion for getting lost.

Who is ultimately responsible?
How can our young compan-
ions be left in charge when the
danger of being left behind is
so real?

Sometimes the
families will return
and search for hours
to try and dry the
tears.

At a *total*
loss

Lost & Found
POLICY

All bears
not claimed
within 30 days
will be
permanently
removed

STUFFING ROOM →

Orsapaedic Hospital

A teddy's life has its share of occupational hazards, but we really don't mind. True, sometimes our injuries result from rough play, but usually they are just the wear and tear of very close contact and a job well done.

Sometimes the *waiting* is

unbearable.

NOSE IDENTIFICATION CHART

BASED ON THE

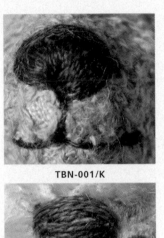

TBN-001/K

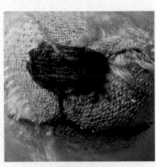

TBN-002/P

TBN-003/J

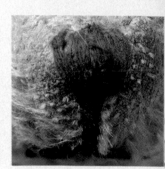

TBN-004/Y

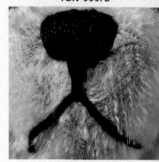

TBN-005/B

TBN-011/K

TBN-012/P

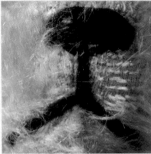

TBN-013/J

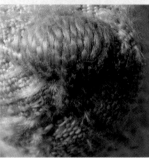

TBN-014/Y

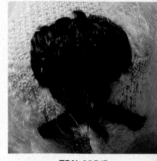

TBN-015/B

TBN-021/K

TBN-022/P

TBN-023/J

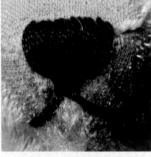

TBN-024/Y

TBN-025/B

TBN-031/K

TBN-032/P

TBN-033/J

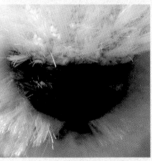

TBN-034/Y

TBN-035/B

TBF-001/Color scale 01

TBF-089/Color scale 02

TBF-112/Color scale 03

TBF-193/Color scale 04

TBF-257/Color scale 05

AND **FUR** TEXTURE/COLOR SCALE

DE VRIES/BAAN PRINCIPLE

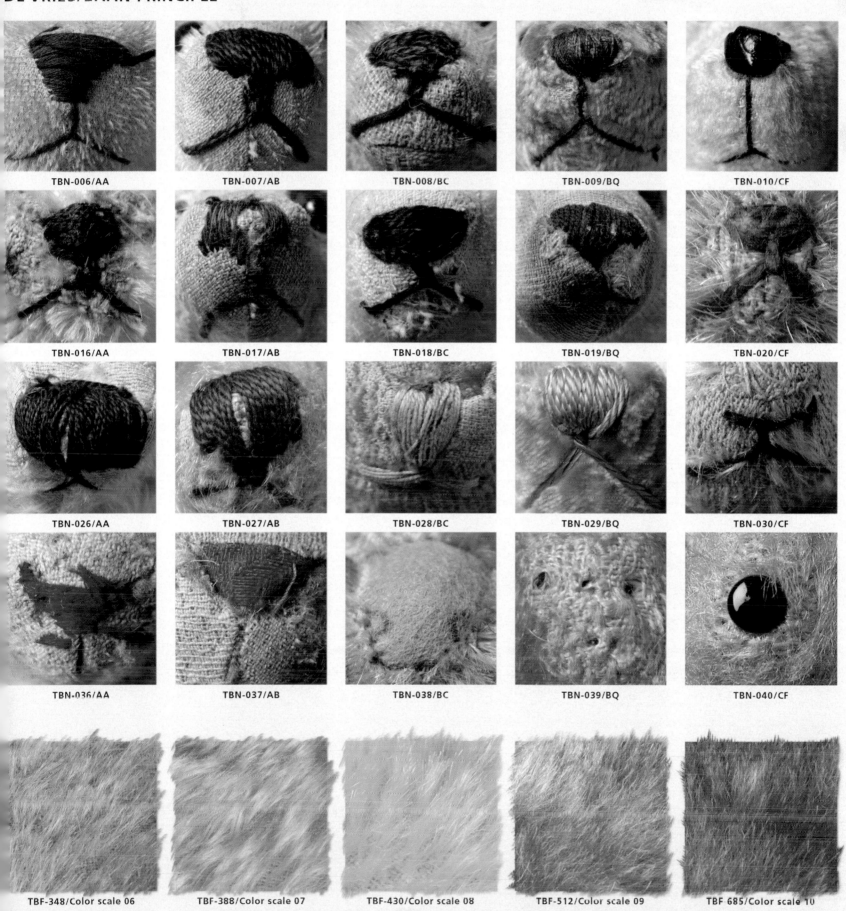

TBN-006/AA TBN-007/AB TBN-008/BC TBN-009/BQ TBN-010/CF

TBN-016/AA TBN-017/AB TBN-018/BC TBN-019/BQ TBN-020/CF

TBN-026/AA TBN-027/AB TBN-028/BC TBN-029/BQ TBN-030/CF

TBN-036/AA TBN-037/AB TBN-038/BC TBN-039/BQ TBN-040/CF

TBF-348/Color scale 06 TBF-388/Color scale 07 TBF-430/Color scale 08 TBF-512/Color scale 09 TBF 685/Color scale 10

"As good as new... wouldn't you agree?"

Of course, the doctor asked why we keep going back.
"Is that a rhetorical question?" I replied. "We return without a moment's
hesitation. What else would you have us do? We're *teddy* bears.
Perhaps you don't understand the depth of this relationship.
Yes, it has happened before, but they promised it won't happen again."

BEAR OUTings

Teddy bears get to travel a lot. Where our companions
go, we go. And whether we actually sit on a sandy beach
or just pretend in a sand box, we enjoy great adventures
in many places...

Camping in the woods or lolling on the grass with
Mama Bear at a picnic spread for family and friends,
sailing, rowing or catching a ride on the back of a duck,
or just taking a nap – that's a bear's idea of a perfect day.
Then, casting our lines by the rapids, we watch the great
Brown Bear catch jumping fish for his dinner.

Gliding in the air, we can see the whole world below.
Singing songs, we go a-hiking into the rugged hills and
climb up to the snowcapped summits with cords and
picks, but some take the cable car up the slopes to snow
country. From there it's merrily, merrily all the way down,
skating, skiing, or sledding past a Panda nibbling on
bamboo – which reminds us that it's time we got back
home where the table is spread with hot chocolate
and honey buns.

Then, "Hold it...smile..." Click, click, click goes the camera
for snapshots to place in an album or send to friends for
the holidays. Teddy bears want to remember everything
about having fun.

Bears in the *wild*…

We do like our bearberries…

For **us** little **pandas**,
finally **finding** a **live** bear
in **black** and white
dispelled our **fears**
of *not* fitting in.

BOOT '90

BU 210

Water play means sailing,
soaring, and
staying afloat – even on a duck...

the afternoon nap...

We can fish like the pros –
                without ever getting wet!

Bears are natural climbers.

We like to get to high places.

Even in winter, some bears
prefer *hiking* to hibernation.

Some of us are *real* snow bears.

The **sporting** life bears lots of fun.

Bearing glad tidings...
Most teddies meet their companions
during the holidays.
It is, therefore, a special and intimate
time for us – a real celebration.

Dear Teddy,

Since Dr. Pill agreed with my parents that you should not accompany me to college, I am making my way on my own.

But I'll be home for the holidays, and we'll be together then.

— Your old friend

Come to the Bear Circus!

Step right up and get your tickets, Mr. and Mrs. Bear, and all you little cubs! Come see the greatest show on Earth!

The colorful clown steps into the ring with the acrobatic mice and monkey to make the audience laugh. Look up from the stands and see the daring young bear on the flying trapeze, leaping and tumbling and flying in mid-air, he's caught in the nick of time by his partner, swinging back and forth. Oh, look at the three funny little bears riding on the back of a donkey. Wait until he starts kicking and running round and round the ring. They'll be shaking up and down and hanging on for dear life as their heads start to spin.

Hey, let's join the circus and live for the center ring!
We'll travel in the circus wagons rolling across the countryside and take care of all the other animals – the mice, the monkey, the donkey and a dog. When we arrive, everybody helps drive the stakes into the ground to hold the tent firmly in place, then hoists the big top up the center pole. Slowly the magic comes back inside the tent, at night, when the teddy bears come rushing in, and the lights are turned up bright, the colorful costumes are put on, the music starts and the show begins.
   Oh, for the life of the circus!

The mice are *especially* entertaining!

The Flying Bing Brothers...
They take the fun
to great heights.

Mirja de Vries gratefully acknowledges the following arctophiles…

*"Thanks to their generous cooperation, advice and support, I was able to photograph the more than 3000 images that helped create **Teddy's World**."*

Jan van der Wal & Jack Freeke
Their teddy bear collection in a cozy canal house
in Amsterdam got me started.
Anne-Marie van Gelder
who entrusted me with her beautiful old Steiff
bears seen in some countryside scenes.
Lyda Rijs-Gertenbach
and Nico – dear friends. Lyda's own "Lyda's Bear"
appears in the mountain and snow scenes
Michel Kracht
and his delightful Teddy Bear collection
Gerrie Schipper
whose personal Teddy Bear collection is
the largest I've ever seen.

Els Roos
always willing to lend me her dearest
Irene Uitermark-Dubach
and her well-loved collection
Door van Ort
whose humorous Schuco bears I photographed
with great pleasure.
Ian Pout
keeper of the magical "Alfonzo," and a very
welcoming shop in Witney, UK.
Ingrid Boom
the Dutch "Teddy Bear Lady"
Eric Giovannini
and his apartment full of teddies

Bob Westerdorp
my assistant/stylist in Teddy Bear Affairs. I benefit-
ted greatly from his perpetual good humor.
Lydia Ferrageau de St. Amand
who made adorable Teddy Bear clothes for me.

And thanks to: Jonette Stabbert, Karin Burema,
Ineke van Zuylen, Kiok Siem, Saskia Voorbach,
Gerda Hinse, Paul Mijksenaar, Ted Badoux,
Tom Benavente, and Ko van Reenen, whose
wonderful bears I photographed.
Also to Beatrijs van Westerop, Heather, Pat Rush,
Jos Smit, Amerongen Castle, Boudewijn Bjelke,
Donna and Boas, for their advice and support.

Joost Elffers would like to thank…

Mark Epstein for introducing me to the work of D.W. Winnicott, whose book
Playing and Reality identifies the teddy bear (and other stuffed animals) as a
transitional object, the first "not me." Winnicott's research confirmed my ideas
for this book and enabled it to go full circle.
Mary Ellen Mark for making a terrific portrait of me and teddy.
Jane Lahr for seeing the great potential and promoting it so well.

Maya Gottfried for her publicity vision.
Linda Stormes for her trade retail expertise.
Marjolijn de Jager for translating some thoughts from Dutch to English.
Andreas Landshoff for his advice and encouragement.
And my family, **Pat Steir** and **Lily Cohen**, whom I terrorized with bear facts
and more for two years.

Teddy Bear Credits

Collection Ted Badoux: 183; **Beerbericht, "Nightwatch"** *from Dutch Teddy Bear Magazine "Beerbericht":* 36-37; **Collection Bontekoe; Teddy Bear Festival Amerongen Castle 1991:** 56-57, 64-65; **Collection Ingrid Boom:** 134; **Collection Joost Elffers:** 94-95; **Collection Anne-Marie van Gelder:** 12, 170-171; **Eric Giovannini's Bears** (www.ericgiovannini.com): 19, 104-105; **Collection Maria de Haan;** *Collection Mossbear:* 8; "De Haven Originals", *Artist bear by Marcha de Haven:* 114; **Collection Gerda Hinse:** 175; **Collection Michel Kracht:** 7, 13-14, 21, 90-91, 115, 174, 176, 181-183; **Collection Paul Mijksenaar:** 80; **Collection Door van Oort:** 31-34, 144-145, 164, 172-173, 176-177, 179, 181; **Collection Ian Pout:** 30, 78-80, 108-109;

Collection Ko van Reenen: 122-123, 126-127; **Collection Lyda Rijs-Gertenbach:** 21, 29, 58, 173, 176; "Lyda's Bear", *Artist bears designed and handmade by Lyda Rijs-Gertenbach:* 69, 76-77, 146, 154-160, 163, 166-167; **Collection Els Roos:** 5, 25, 29, 35, 39, 78, 87, 96-97, 99-103, 110-111, 161, 168-171, 180; **Collection Gerrie Schipper:** 22, 25, 81-87, 94-95, 115, 150-151; **Collection Kiok Siem:** 162; **Jonette Stabbert,** *Bears designed and handmade by Jonette Stabbert:* 148-149; **Collection Irene Uitermark-Dubach:** 10-11, 139, 142-143; **Collection Mirja de Vries:** 16-17, 31-34, 40-43, 58-60, 67, 106-107, 120-123, 130, 135-138, 171-172; **Collection Jan van der Wal:** 118-119

Photograph Credits

Polar Bear Cover Photos / Polar Bear Paws in Tank (p. 15) / **Polar Bear Swimming in Tank** (pp. 16-17) **Images photographed at Lincoln Park Zoo, Chicago, Illinois © Todd Rosenberg**
Brown Bear in Water (p. 18) / **Brown Bears Fishing in Falls** (pp. 152-153) **© Kennan Ward/Corbis**
Bear Diorama (pp. 20-21) / **Bear image in Folder** (p. 22) / **Bear Bear image on poster** (p. 24) **Collection of The Museum of Natural History, New York, NY USA**
Bones of a Polar Bear by Waterhouse Hawkins, 19th Century (p. 23) **Oxford Museum of Natural History, UK/Bridgeman Art Library**

Detail of Mosaic Depicting Circus Games (pp. 24, 26-27) **Image photographed at the Tripoli Museum, Libya. © Roger Wood/Corbis**
The Bear Dance by William H. Beard, oil, 1879 (p. 28) / *Bulls and Bears in the Market* by William H. Beard, oil, 1879 (p. 29) **Collection of The New York Historical Society, New York, USA/Bridgeman Art Library**
Nightwatch by Rembrandt (pp. 36-37) **Collection of Rijksmuseum Amsterdam**
Jongeling met Beer by A. Hondius (pp. 30-31) **Private Collection**
Photos (pp. 52, 68-69, 92) **Joost Guntenaar, Amsterdam**

Salmon Movie Cartoon (p. 53) © **The New Yorker Collection 1989 Warren Miller from cartoonbank.com. All rights reserved.**
Garbage Cartoon (p. 53) © **The New Yorker Collection 2001 Mike Twohy from cartoonbank.com. All rights reserved.**
Photos (pp. 61-63, 79, 123) **Michiel Kracht**
Photos (pp. 78-80, 109) **Collection of Ian Pout, Witney, England**
Original Wallpapers (pp. 98-99, 128-129) **Collection Koops-Marcus, Amsterdam**
Giant Panda Eating Bamboo (pp. 144-145) / **Giant Panda Lying in Snow** (pp. 164-165) © **Keren Su/Corbis**

Credits

Photography, styling, and concepts
Mirja de Vries*
(27 years of teddy bear photographs/archives)

Concepts, script and storyboard; sketches
Joost Elffers*

Editorial Board
Mirja de Vries, Joost Elffers,
Erik Thé, Iwan Baan

Art Director
Erik Thé

Art Composer; photography
Iwan Baan

Text Editor
Lindy Judge

Introduction Editor
Charles Ruas*

Design Assistant
Brigitte Hendrix

Image Research
Anne Lammers

Creative Digital Imaging Consultant
Michiel Hofmans

Office Manager
Radha Pancham

Model Maker
Boudewijn Bjelke

Lithographic Art Composer
Max Köcher

Lithographer
Litho Köcher GmbH, Cologne

Printer
Druckerei Uhl, Radolfzell am Bodensee

* Arctophile

SAEVIS INTER SE CONVENIT URSIS
(Bears live in harmony with bears)

The Last Word

"Now that the day is done, let's sit here, you and I, in this spot where bears like to be just looking at the world rolling away from our feet. Let's talk of children who have outgrown their bears, and of bears sitting on a shelf or wrapped away in a trunk, waiting for a new child friend to come and take them on another journey into the world."

"A childhood passes in the blink of an eye, but the bear is still as good as new."

"Have you ever thought of all the countless bears who are forgotten and no longer needed? Have you asked yourself what will happen to them?"

"Yes. Sometimes they meet up with people who have lost their beloved teddy bears or had them cruelly taken away when they were still very young, but have never stopped looking for their lost bear. Or maybe they're people who never even had their own bear. When they grew up, they still feel the need and must go on searching for their bear. So, they adopt all the lost bears they encounter on their way in life. They become Aunts and Uncles of all these lost teddy bears."

"They run orphanages for homeless old bears that sometimes become so large they turn into Bear Collections or even Bear Museums."

"And these Aunts and Uncles wake up in the morning needing to find more bears. They send them to the doctor to be repaired, and they spend so much time caring and cleaning and dressing them up as good as new again that the bear hardly gets any sleep at all. At times they can be a bit overbearing. They bring the bears together to play, and their homes become filled to bursting with frolicking teddy bears. Some particularly important, famous or beautiful bears are put on display so that their child friends can come and admire them, and love them again – but only through the glass of their cases."

"But when do they go into the world again to live the life of a child?"

"Oh, they never ever leave that world. Whenever they settle down in a bear spot as peaceful as this, bears will open their hearts and tell about their adventures with their child friends. But don't forget, what the child sees the bear sees, and we know that bears live on hope. So, anytime they wish, bears can go right back to life with a child friend. That's the particular power of Teddy Bears."

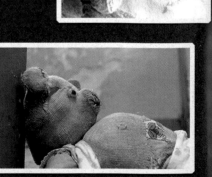